winter
sports

English translation © Copyright 1992 by Barron's Educational Series, Inc.

© Parramón Ediciones, S.A.
Published by Parramón Ediciones, S.A., Barcelona, Spain
The title of the Spanish edition is *Los deportes en la nieve.*
Author: Isidro Sánchez; illustrator: Carme Peris; translated from the
Spanish by Edith Wilson

All inquiries should be addressed to:
Barron's Educational Series, Inc.
250 Wireless Boulevard
Hauppauge, New York 11788

Library of Congress Catalog Card No. 91-32927

International Standard Book No. 0-8120-4868-7

Library of Congress Cataloging-in-Publication Data
Sánchez, Isidro.
  [Deportes en la nieve.   English]
  Winter sports / Isidro Sánchez, Carme Peris ;—[translated from the
Spanish by Edith Wilson].
    p.   cm. — (The World of sports)
  Translation of: Los deportes en la nieve.
  Summary: Briefly describes some of the activities that can be
enjoyed in the snow, such as making a snowman, sledding, snow-
mobiling, and skiing.
  ISBN 0-8120-4868-7
  1. Winter sports—Juvenile literature. [1. Winter sports. 2. Skis
and skiing.] I. Peris, Carme, ill. II. Title. III. Series: Sánchez,
Isidro. World of sports.
GV841.S2513   1992
796.9—dc20   91-32927
                                              CIP
                                              AC

Printed in Spain
2345   0987654321

the world of sports

winter sports

Isidro Sánchez

Carme Peris

BARRON'S

At the ski resort, we will all have fun skiing and playing in the snow.

Fortunately, we are wearing our warm clothing. As soon as we arrive, it starts to snow. I love to play in the snow!

Some of the children are having a
snowball fight. We help make a
snowman and wrap a colorful scarf
around his neck to keep him warm.

Ice-skating is also great fun. We fall down a lot, but it never seems to hurt!

I sit behind my brother and we have an exciting race on our sleds.

Fast, faster…zoom! Down the hill we go!

A cable car takes us to the top of the ski slope.

Our big moment is almost here!

Our instructor shows us how to hold the ski poles and line up our skis. It is really not hard to learn when someone helps us.

A ski lift carries the more experienced skiers to the steeper slopes. We wave to them as they pass us.

We stop on the slope to watch some skiing competitions. Mom explains that the ski jumpers try to land as far away as they can to win the contest. They are also judged on their form.

In the slalom race, the skiers need to be quick at making turns so they can pass between the flags.

The cross-country competition tests the skiers' endurance over a long, snow-covered course.

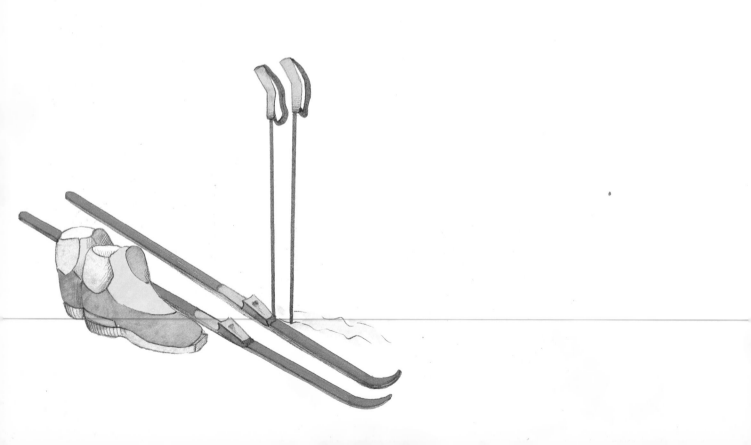

The snowmobiles come racing down the slope at full speed.

"Come on! Come on!" I cheer excitedly for my favorite driver.

We get ready for the trip back home.
Mom puts the skis on the ski rack,
while Dad fits the chains on the tires
to keep the car from skidding.

We are sad to leave the ski resort
because we had so much fun!

WINTER SPORTS

The "Wooden Plank"

The name ski derives from a Norwegian word that means "wooden plank" and today defines not only devices used to glide through the snow, but also the sport itself.

The invention of these "wooden planks" predates their use in games. Skis evolved from the need to travel on snow-covered trails, which were a challenge to the survival of people in the northern latitudes.

By the second half of the nineteenth century, skiing competitions, such as those we see today, were popular in Norway. Skiing as a sport spread from Scandinavia to the Alpine countries—first to Switzerland, and later to Austria, Germany, France, and Italy.

At the beginning of the twentieth century, skiing was already an established sport in virtually all of Europe, as well as in the United States, Canada, and Australia. Moreover, it had formed its own national and international organizations to promote the sport.

Techniques and Equipment

Modern skiing techniques achieve maximum control of the skis through the skier's body movements and alternate shifting of body weight.

Along with the evolution of techniques, skiing equipment has advanced in shape design and construction materials, which vary according to the skiing specialty involved. For instance, cross-country skis, which are relatively long, are only 2 to 2½ inches (5–6 cm) wide and curved at the tips; downhill skis are laminated with plastic and are 3 to 5 inches (7–10 cm) wide; jumping skis can be more than 8 feet (2.4 m) long and measure 5 inches (12 cm) in width.

Competitive Skiing

Skiing competitions comprise two specialties: (1) Nordic events (the original form), which include cross-country races, relay races, jumping, the Nordic Combined, and the Biathlon; (2) Alpine events (a later addition), which involve downhill races, slalom, giant slalom, and the Alpine Combined.

Nordic Events

Cross-country races unfold along a course that is 3 to 31 miles (10–50 km) long, depending on the category. Competitors ski over a rolling terrain that encompasses equal stretches of downgrades, upgrades, and flat ground.

Relay races are a variation of cross-country events. Teams of three to four people compete against each other.

In ski jumping, the length of the jump is measured from the end of the slope to the jumper's landing site. In this event, other elements besides the length of the jump are considered—for example, the style displayed at the start and all throughout the execution of the jump.

The Nordic Combined competition consists of a cross-country run and a ski jump.

The Biathlon is a cross-country race that also requires its competitors to stop at several predetermined ranges to fire a rifle at a target.

Alpine Events

Downhill races are run on slopes 1 to 2 miles (2–3 km) long with a descent of less than 3,281 (1,000 m) feet. A downhill skier can easily exceed a speed of 60 miles (100 km) per hour.

In the slalom race, the skiers must pass through a series of gates, consisting of two flags placed 10 to 13 feet (3.2–4 m) apart, that test the turning skill of the racers. There are two legs to this race. Although the course is the same length in both legs, each leg is laid out differently. The time for each run is tallied for the final score.

The giant slalom event differs from the slalom only in length. The course may be up to 1 1/2 miles (2.5 km) long.

The Alpine Combined is a contest that combines a downhill race with a slalom or giant slalom.

On the Ice

A winter sport that has gained enormous popularity due to the Olympics is figure skating. The categories include male and female solo performances, pairs, and ice dancing. Competitors are judged according to their grace and athleticism. Speed skating, always popular in the Netherlands, has also become popular throughout most of the world.

Sledding

Other enjoyable winter activities that have become Olympic sports include bobsledding, in which two or more people sit on a large sled that is equipped with two pairs of runners, a steering wheel, and hand brake; and luge, in which the competitor rides lying down on a specially designed sled.

Outdoor Winter Activities for the Child

Outdoor exercise is essential to the physical development of a young child. Aside from improving muscle coordination, skiing can stimulate discovery of the natural environment and introduce movements that are different from those learned by children in their everyday activities.

Read and Think Questions for Children

1. What have the children used to make the snowman's nose? Does the snowman need a scarf to keep warm? What do you think will happen to the snowman if the sun comes out and warms up the day?

2. Why are the children falling down on the ice? Do you think it hurts to fall? Why are the children still smiling?

3. Why are the children riding in a cable car? Why don't they just walk up the mountain?

4. Why do the children need goggles and poles when they are skiing?

5. What are the different kinds of skiing competitions the children watch? Which one do you think you would like best?